A Note to Parents and Teachers

DK READERS is a compelling program for beginning readers, designed in conjunction with leading literacy experts, including Dr. Linda Gambrell, director of the Eugene T. Moore School of Education, Clemson University, and past president of the National Reading Conference.

Beautiful illustrations and superb full-color photographs combine with engaging, easy-to-read stories to offer a fresh approach to each subject in the series. Each DK READER is guaranteed to capture a child's interest while developing his or her reading skills, general knowledge, and love of reading.

The four levels of DK READERS are aimed at different reading abilities, enabling you to choose the books that are exactly right for your child:

Level 1 – Beginning to read
Level 2 – Beginning to read alone
Level 3 – Reading alone
Level 4 – Proficient readers

The "normal" age at which a child begins to read can be anywhere from three to eight years old, so these levels are only a general guideline.

No matter which level you select, you can be sure that you are helping your child learn to read, then read to learn!

LONDON, NEW YORK, MUNICH,
MELBOURNE, AND DELHI

Senior Editor Beth Sutinis
Senior Art Editor Michelle Baxter
Publisher Chuck Lang
Creative Director Tina Vaughan
Production Chris Avgherinos

Reading Consultant
Linda Gambrell, Ph.D.

Produced by
Shoreline Publishing Group
Editorial Director James Buckley, Jr.
Art Director Tom Carling,
Carling Design, Inc.

Produced in partnership and licensed by
Major League Baseball Properties, Inc.
Vice President of Publishing
Don Hintze

First American Edition, 2003

03 04 05 10 9 8 7 6 5 4 3 2 1
Published in the United States by DK Publishing, Inc.
375 Hudson St., New York, NY 10014

Published in Great Britain by Dorling Kindersley Limited

A catalog record is available from the Library of Congress.

0-7894-9251-2 (PB)
0-7894-9545-7 (HC)

Color reproduction by Colourscan, Singapore
Printed and bound in China by L Rex Printing Co., Ltd.

Photography credits:
All photos courtesy of Major League Baseball Photos and the National Baseball Hall of Fame and Library except the following: AP/Wide World: 26b, 27tr, 29, 30, 36; Corbis: 18t, 18b, 22b; DK Publishing: 13t, 26t, 27t, 30t.

Discover more at
www.dk.com

Contents

THE STORY OF THE NEW YORK YANKEES

Written by David Fischer

DK Publishing, Inc.

Superstar
The great slugger Babe Ruth is one of 33 Yankees in the Hall of Fame. That total is more than any other team.

Famous logo
The top hat in the Yankees' All-American logo is modeled after the one worn by Uncle Sam.

Who are the Yankees?

From their beginnings in 1903 until today, the Yankees have been baseball's most successful team. The Yankees have won more league pennants (38) and more World Series (26) than any other team in Major League Baseball history. The Yankees are the only team ever to win five World Series in a row (1949–1953) and the only team ever to win four World Series in a row (1936–1939). They also won four of five World Series from 1996 to 2000.

From the glory of Babe Ruth and the pride of Lou Gehrig, to the grace of Joe DiMaggio and the sheer power of Mickey Mantle, to the reign of today's World Series heroes—Derek Jeter, Bernie Williams, Jorge Posada, Tino Martinez, and Mariano Rivera—the Yankees are baseball's most famous team.

Year after year, the Yankees have fielded the best team in baseball. This is the story of their incredible success.

Celebrate!
Scott Brosius (18) and Mariano Rivera (42) jumped for joy in 2000 when the Yankees won another title.

Hardware
This is the current version of the World Series trophy. The Yankees have taken home more of these than any other team. The gold flags represent baseball's 30 teams.

A.L. founder
Ban Johnson owned the Chicago White Sox and founded the American League in 1901.

Early ace
Pitcher Jack Chesbro was one of the Highlanders' few stars. He led the A.L. with 41 wins in 1904

The early years

The American League (A.L.) was brand new in 1901. Its president, Bancroft "Ban" Johnson, knew that to compete against the older National League (N.L.), the A.L. would need a team in New York, the nation's largest city. So he moved the Baltimore Orioles to New York City for the 1903 season.

The team played its games in a small wooden ballpark in New York City. That home field, called Hilltop Park, was one of the highest spots in the city, and so the club became known as the New York Highlanders.

First home
Here is a rare 1909 photo showing action at Hilltop Park in New York. Many baseball fields of the time had a dirt strip between the mound and home plate.

During those early years, the team never posed a serious threat in the standings. They never won a pennant, and they finished higher than fourth place only three times. In 1912, the Highlanders finished last, 55 games out of first place.

Babe
He began as a pitcher and became the greatest slugger the game has ever known. Babe Ruth was born in Baltimore in 1895. He signed his first pro contract at 19 with a Baltimore minor-league team.

Team owner
Yankees owner Jacob Ruppert called himself "Colonel" because of his rank in the New York National Guard.

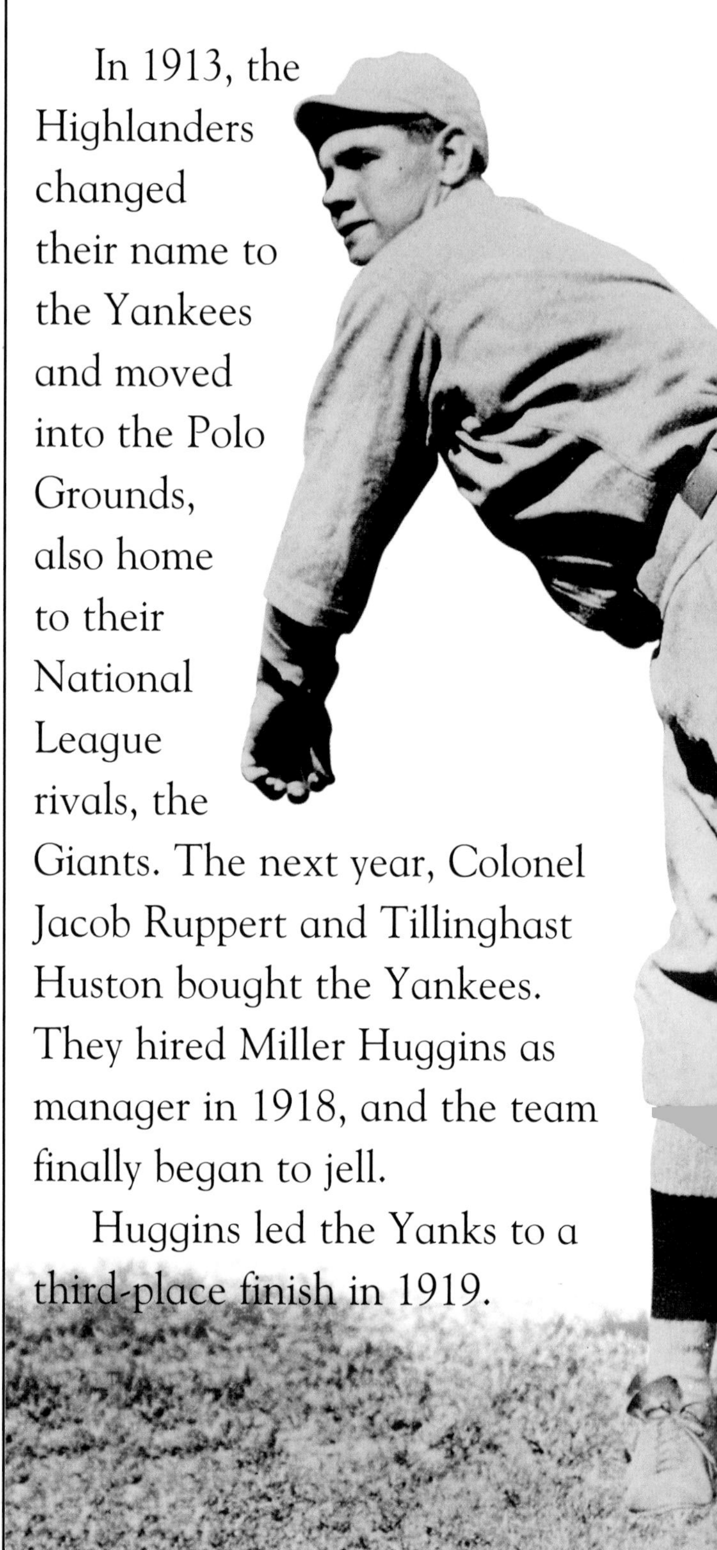

In 1913, the Highlanders changed their name to the Yankees and moved into the Polo Grounds, also home to their National League rivals, the Giants. The next year, Colonel Jacob Ruppert and Tillinghast Huston bought the Yankees. They hired Miller Huggins as manager in 1918, and the team finally began to jell.

Huggins led the Yanks to a third-place finish in 1919.

That year, the Yankees hit more home runs (45) than any other American League club. But a young Boston Red Sox pitcher–outfielder hit 29 homers all by himself. His name was George Herman "Babe" Ruth. Following the 1919 season, Huggins persuaded the Yankees front office to purchase Ruth from the Red Sox. The Babe was acquired for $125,000, and baseball changed forever. Ruth's arrival signaled the beginning of the Yankees dynasty.

Lucky find
Frank "Home Run" Baker earned his nickname in a time when very few homers were hit. Until Babe Ruth came along, Baker was the best long-ball hitter, with three league home-run titles. He was first called "Home Run" after hitting a pair in the 1911 World Series.

New ball
Beginning with the 1920 season, the A.L. and N.L. used a new ball. The "lively" ball traveled farther, making homers more frequent.

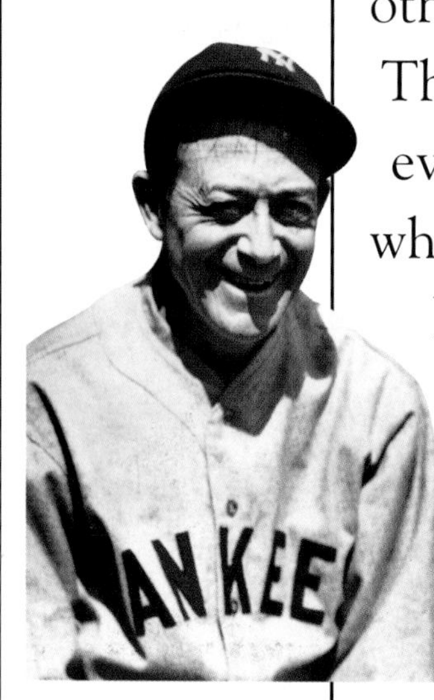

Mighty Mite
Though very short and small, manager Miller Huggins was the big man in the Yankee clubhouse. He kept Ruth in line and led the team to six A.L. pennants.

Babe and Lou

The Yankees made Babe Ruth a starter in the outfield, and he had an immediate impact. The player they would call "the Sultan of Swat" smashed a mind-boggling 54 home runs in 1920—more than any other *team* in the league!

The next year "the Bambino" did even better, belting 59 homers, while the batter with the next highest home-run total that year hit 24. From 1926 through 1931, Ruth averaged more than 50 home runs a year!

Spurred on by his fantastic long balls, fans flocked to ballparks to watch the Babe in action. The Yankees built a new stadium to hold the crowds that came to see him. The big ballpark in the Bronx was called Yankee Stadium, but sportswriters dubbed it "the House That Ruth Built."

When Yankee Stadium opened on April 23, 1923, Ruth hit the first home run there. Ruth led the league in home runs that season and the Yankees won their first World Series championship.

Home in the Bronx
Yankee Stadium is located on the East River in the Bronx section of New York City.

Whiff!
Babe Ruth smashed 714 home runs in his career, but he also missed the ball a lot, too! When he retired in 1935, his 1,330 strikeouts were the most ever. Since then many modern players have passed him.

What a pair! Both Gehrig and Ruth were lefthanded hitters, but they were very different people. Ruth (right) was loud and outgoing, Gehrig was quiet and more private.

Lou Gehrig became the starting first baseman in 1926, and from then until 1932, he and Ruth were the two greatest hitters ever to play together. Ruth and Gehrig finished first and second, respectively, in the home-run race each season from 1927 to 1931.

The Yankees won the A.L. pennant in 1926, 1927, 1928, and 1932. They swept the World Series in three of those seasons.

The 1927 Yankees won 110 games, an American League record that lasted for 27 years. The Yanks lineup was called “Murderers’ Row” because of the way they terrorized opposing pitchers. The heart of the order—Ruth, Gehrig, left fielder Bob Meusel, and second baseman Tony Lazzeri—all drove in more than 100 runs each. The team average was .307. Ruth became the first man ever to hit 60 home runs in a season. No batter would match Ruth’s mark for 34 seasons!

Good seats
Writers who covered the 1927 World Series were given this gold pin, which allowed them into the locker room and onto the field to interview players.

Second sacker
While Ruth and Gehrig got the headlines, Tony Lazzeri was one of several other Yankees who were great players. In 1936, he became the first player to hit two grand slams in one game.

The pitching wasn't bad either. In 1927, Waite Hoyt led the league with 22 wins, Herb Pennock and Wilcey Moore each won 19, and Urban Shocker won 18. The 1927 Yankees—considered by many to be the best team ever—beat the Pittsburgh Pirates in the World Series.

Series slugger Babe Ruth hit 15 home runs in World Series play, the second most of all time.

Success on and off the field After finishing his Hall of Fame career, Waite Hoyt became a successful businessman and later broadcast Cincinnati Reds games.

The next year, they did the same against the St. Louis Cardinals.

The Yankees returned to the Series in 1932, against the Chicago Cubs. Babe Ruth's most famous homer came in Game Three of that Series. Babe is said to have pointed at the centerfield bleachers in Chicago's Wrigley Field before belting a long home run to that exact spot.

Did Ruth "call" his home run—did he really predict that he would hit it? No one knows for sure. He may have been pointing to the pitcher, or showing the crowd that he still had one more strike. Another possibility is that he might have been gesturing at the Cubs bench, which was filled with players who were teasing him. Still, Babe's "Called Shot" remains one of the most legendary home runs in World Series history.

Beat the Yanks Former Phillies' pitcher Grover Cleveland Alexander led the Cardinals to an upset win over the Yankees in the 1926 Series.

Ace catcher Hall of Fame catcher Bill Dickey was a key part of Yankees teams

Great moment Cal Ripken, Jr. of the Baltimore Orioles broke Gehrig's record for consecutive games in 1995.

Great leader Joe McCarthy managed the Yanks from 1931 to 1946 and won a record seven World Series.

If Ruth was a roller-coaster ride, Gehrig was smooth and steady. He became known as "the Iron Horse" by playing in an incredible 2,130 games in a row. Gehrig combined his dependability with one of the greatest bats in baseball history.

Because his home runs didn't travel as far as Ruth's, Gehrig's productive career is often overlooked. Lou knocked in more than 100 runs for 13 straight seasons, topping 150 Runs Batted In seven times and setting the A.L. record with 184 in 1931. He won the Triple Crown twice. And on June 3, 1932, Gehrig became the first American League player to hit four home runs in one game.

Smart guy
Gehrig had attended Columbia University in New York. When he joined the Yankees, he was one of only a handful of players who had gone to college.

Soon Ruth's power was to fade, and the Iron Horse would take center stage. Gehrig won the Triple Crown in 1934, leading the league in batting average (.363), homers (49), and RBI (165). That year was also Ruth's last with the Yankees.

Rookie
A rookie is a major-league professional athlete in his first season in the sport. Most baseball rookies make the majors after playing in the minor leagues.

Out West
Joe DiMaggio was born in San Francisco and was a star for the minor-league San Francisco Seals.

A rookie named Joe DiMaggio joined the club in 1936. He and Gehrig became as fearsome a one-two punch as Ruth and Gehrig had been. Between 1936 and 1939, the Yankees were almost unbeatable, averaging 100 victories and winning four consecutive World Series.

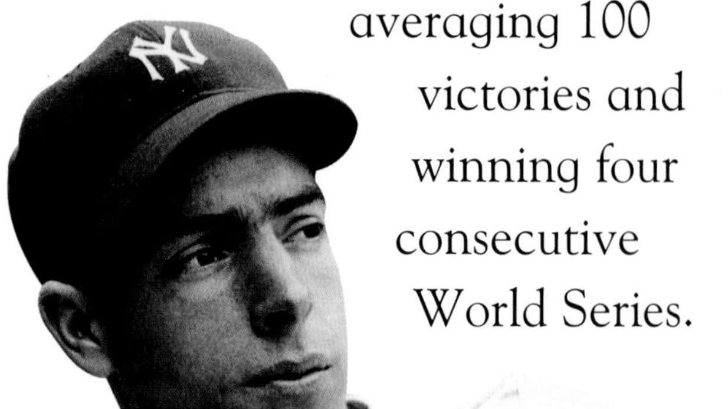

In 1938, Gehrig's batting average fell below .300 for the first time since 1925; something was obviously wrong. Gehrig took himself out of the lineup on May 2, 1939. Lou would soon learn that he had an incurable disease known as amyotrophic lateral sclerosis (ALS), which crippled his nerves and muscles.

The illness, which came to be called "Lou Gehrig's disease," forced him to retire. On July 4, 1939, the Yanks held Lou Gehrig Day and nearly 62,000 fans came to Yankee Stadium to honor him. Later that year, the great first baseman was elected to the Baseball Hall of Fame. He died just two years later.

A saddened nation and grieving Yankees team headed into a difficult decade without the Iron Horse.

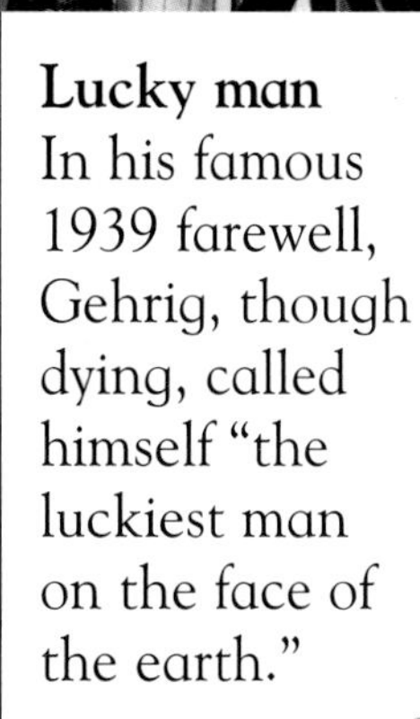

Lucky man
In his famous 1939 farewell, Gehrig, though dying, called himself "the luckiest man on the face of the earth."

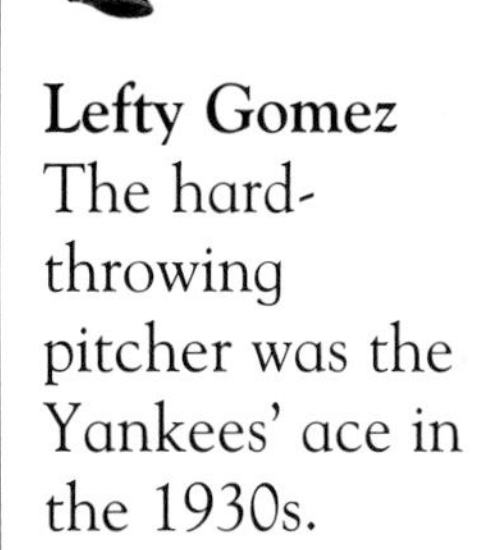

Lefty Gomez
The hard-throwing pitcher was the Yankees' ace in the 1930s.

Super slugger Boston's Ted Williams and DiMaggio often were 1 and 2 in the MVP voting.

Close but... Pete Rose came close to DiMaggio's record with a 44-game streak in 1978.

War and a dynasty

Like his idol Lou Gehrig, Joe DiMaggio was a quiet man who led by example. He was named most valuable player in 1939, 1941, and 1947. In 1941, he completed one of baseball's most amazing feats. From May to July of that year he hit safely in a record 56 consecutive games.

Joe's streak began on May 15 with a single off White Sox pitcher Edgar Smith. Over the next two months, he had at least one base hit in every game he played. During that time, he batted .408 with 15 homers and 55 RBI. Each day, Americans would check their newspapers for news about World War II.... and to see if "Joltin' Joe" got another hit.

The streak finally ended on July 17, in a game against the Cleveland Indians.

He kept it going
After his streak was ended in July 1941, DiMaggio then had a hit in 16 more games in a row. All together, he had a hit in 72 out of 73 games, a record that will probably never be broken.

Old days
This picture of Joe DiMaggio at bat shows a few things that were different in the "old days." Notice that the uniforms were much baggier. Players also did not wear batting helmets or batting gloves.

Joe's nickname Thanks to his smooth fielding style, DiMaggio was known as "the Yankee Clipper," a pun on the name of an old-time sailing ship.

Army man Here is Sgt. Joe DiMaggio receiving a decoration during World War II.

The Yankees were now DiMaggio's team, and they didn't miss a beat. In 1941, the Yanks returned to the Series and beat the Brooklyn Dodgers in five games. The Yanks lost to the St. Louis Cardinals in 1942, but avenged that loss the next season, whipping the Cards in five games. It had been an impressive run for the Bronx Bombers—seven A.L. pennants and six world championships in eight seasons.

As it turned out, only World War II could slow the Yankees juggernaut. DiMaggio and many other great stars of the game went into military service and missed several seasons while serving their country. DiMaggio returned in 1946 and was the Most Valuable Player (MVP) in '47. That year, he led the Yankees to another championship under new manager Bucky Harris. The 1947 Series, a tight seven-game triumph over the Brooklyn Dodgers, was memorable for the heartbreak felt by Yankee pitcher Bill Bevens. He lost Game Four despite being one out away from throwing the first no-hitter in World Series history.

So close—and yet so far
In Bill Bevens's famous near no-hitter in 1947, he lost the game and the record by giving up a hit to Cookie Lavagetto in the ninth inning after walking two Dodgers batters.

Two of a kind
The Yankees' greatest rival over the years has been the Boston Red Sox. That team's biggest star, Ted Williams, here with DiMaggio, was perhaps the best hitter of all time—but he couldn't help the Red Sox beat the Yankees.

Made a point
Casey Stengel was known as "the Old Perfessor" for his baseball smarts and wacky way of talking.

Reynolds rap
Allie Reynolds pitched for the Yankees from 1947 to 1954 and became one of its greatest aces. He won seven World Series games.

Casey Stengel, a former outfielder, took over as manager in 1949. Right away he faced a challenge when his best player, Joe DiMaggio, was injured.

He missed the first half of the season with a bad heel. He came back in July and hit .346 for the rest of the season. The Yanks edged the Red Sox for the pennant and beat the Dodgers in the World Series.

In 1950, the Yanks swept the Phillies for their thirteenth world title. Shortstop Phil Rizzuto earned the MVP award. “Scooter” played in 10 World Series during his 13-year career with the Yanks, and was Series MVP in 1951.

DiMaggio played his last game in the 1951 Series, closing out a legendary career on a winning note, driving in five runs as the Yankees beat the New York Giants in six games. In Joe’s 13 seasons, the Yanks won nine World Series.

Series kids
The 1950 Philadelphia Phillies were known as “the Whiz Kids.”

Second job
After finishing his great Yankee career, shortstop Phil Rizzuto (left) was a longtime broadcaster for the team.

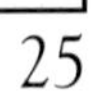

Good ticket
This ticket got a lucky fan into Game Five of the 1956 World Series, one of the most famous games in baseball history.

DiMaggio's replacement in centerfield was a 19-year-old from Oklahoma named Mickey Mantle. He combined awesome power and blinding speed. Mantle was known for his "tape-measure" home runs. One long blast zoomed 565 feet at Washington's Griffith Stadium in 1953. In the 1952 World Series, Mantle blasted the first of his record 18 Series homers. The Yanks won their fifth straight title in 1953, defeating Brooklyn four games to two.

Yankee beater
Milwaukee Braves pitcher Lew Burdette (center) celebrates his third win in the 1957 World Series when the Braves upset the Yanks.

The Bronx Bombers came back to win again in 1956. The highlight was pitcher Don Larsen's perfect game in Game Five, the only one ever in a World Series.

New York's 1958 championship moved Stengel into a tie with Joe McCarthy, who also won seven titles.

Stengel was the most successful skipper in Yankees history. In 12 seasons at the helm, he led the team to ten pennants and seven World Series titles, including the five in a row from 1949 to 1953.

Perfect!
This famous photo shows Yogi Berra leaping into the arms of perfect-game pitcher Don Larsen

What a year!
Mickey Mantle's greatest year was 1956, when he won the Triple Crown. Mantle was also one of baseball's fastest runners. He was called "the Commerce Comet" after his Oklahoma hometown.

Smile, Yogi! Childhood friends gave Lawrence Berra the nickname of "Yogi" after a movie character. Here the Hall of Fame catcher poses for a photo during spring training.

Slugging catcher Cincinnati Reds star Johnny Bench would break many of Berra's hitting records for catchers during his Major League career (1967 to 1983).

One of Stengel's best decisions as a manager was to put Yogi Berra behind the plate as the Yankees catcher starting in 1950. From then until 1957, Berra caught an average of nearly 140 games a season.

He won the MVP award three times (1951, 1954, 1955). Yogi played in more World Series (14) and for more World Series winners than any other player. He holds Series records for most games played (75) and most hits (71), and with 39 RBI he is one behind Mantle for the most all-time.

The 1960 Yankees were formed around a new power duo in the tradition of Ruth and Gehrig, and Gehrig and DiMaggio. Slugging outfielder Roger Maris joined Mantle in the lineup. Maris won the MVP award as the Yanks won yet another A.L. title. In the World Series, however, the Yankees were beaten in the seventh game.

Stengel was fired not long after, but the Yankees dynasty continued.

Yogi
The word yogi (YOH-ghee) means a holy man or person of great learning in India.

Whoo-hoo!
Pirates second baseman Bill Mazeroski rounds the bases after hitting one of the most famous homers ever. His run won the 1960 World Series over New York.

Mr. 61 to Mr. October

The 1961 season was an unforgettably sweet ride. The Yankees won 109 games and stomped on the Cincinnati Reds to win the World Series in five games. The team hit an earthshaking 240 home runs, a record that stood for 34 years. Mantle battled Maris—for a chance to break Babe Ruth's record of 60 home runs in a season.

Big buttons
Yankees fans in 1961 sported buttons like these honoring their two great sluggers.

M&M Boys
Roger Maris was a shy, quiet man from North Dakota who avoided the spotlight. Mickey Mantle, on the other hand, loved making headlines on and off the field.

Mantle started out red-hot, but injuries forced him to drop out of the race with 54 homers. On the final day of the season, Maris connected with a pitch by Boston's Tracey Stallard for home run number 61.

Just as Maris had surpassed Babe's homer record, Whitey Ford knocked Ruth out of the World Series record book. As a Red Sox pitcher, the Babe once pitched 29 consecutive scoreless innings. In 1960, Ford extended his streak to 32 consecutive scoreless innings.

Ford had a 25-4 record during the 1961 season and won the Cy Young Award as the majors' top pitcher. Ford's career record of 236-106 gives him the best career winning percentage (.690) of any pitcher since 1900.

Super in the Series
Whitey Ford holds the all-time World Series career records for most wins (10) and strikeouts (94).

Top pitcher
The Cy Young Award is named for the Hall of Fame pitcher who won a record 511 games.

Great hands
After taking over as the Yankees catcher from Yogi Berra, Elston Howard was nearly his equal. He was a solid hitter and pitchers loved to have him behind the plate.

Mantle won his third MVP award in 1962, and the Yankees won another world championship, this time over the San Francisco Giants. In 1963, the magic spell ended when the Los Angeles Dodgers swept the Yankees in four games. That year the Yankees' first African-American player, catcher Elston Howard, became the fourth Yankee in a row to be named the A.L. MVP. Yogi Berra took over as manager in 1964, but was fired after the Yankees lost the World Series to the St. Louis Cardinals.

The 1964 season would turn out to be the final year of the Yankees dynasty that had started in the 1920s with Babe Ruth. The dynasty had peaked from 1947 to 1964, when the Yankees won 15 American League pennants and 10 World Series crowns. It would be more than a decade before the team would once again be the best.

Despite the efforts of players such as pitcher Mel Stottlemyre and outfielders Bobby Murcer and Roy White, the once-proud Yankees remained out of pennant contention until January 1973. That's when a group of businessmen headed by Cleveland shipbuilder George Steinbrenner purchased the Yankees.

Just missed Though he played on five All-Star teams, Bobby Murcer was never on a Yankees championship team.

In bronze Yankee Stadium's Monument Park is home to bronze plaques honoring great Yankees of the past.

"The Boss"
George Steinbrenner quickly made his way the Yankee way. He didn't mind spending a lot of money to get players, and he had no patience for people who didn't win. Since Steinbrenner bought the Yankees, they have won six World Series titles.

Free agent
Until 1974, baseball teams could hold on to a player for as long as they liked. A court decision in 1974 declared that players could shop their services to any team. These players are known as free agents.

Steinbrenner promised to bring a winner back to the Bronx, no matter how much the cost. He took advantage of baseball's new free-agent system in which players could sign with the highest bidder. Steinbrenner offered pitcher Jim "Catfish" Hunter more than $3 million in 1975. Soon, the Yankees acquired other top players.

The best included Chris Chambliss, Graig Nettles, Willie Randolph, and Lou Piniella. Other young stars included Ron Guidry and Thurman Munson.

Manager Billy Martin led the club into the playoffs against the Kansas City Royals. In the decisive fifth game, Chambliss slugged a dramatic home run in the bottom of the ninth inning, making the Yankees league champions for the first time in over a decade. But Cincinnati's Big Red Machine defeated the Yankees by sweeping the Series in 1976.

New York went shopping again and signed slugger Reggie Jackson. It proved to be a very good move.

Ace hurler
Catfish Hunter helped the Yankees win World Series titles in 1977 and 1978.

Fixer-upper
The Yankees rebuilt their famous stadium in 1976, adding more seats.

Trivia time
Amaze your friends by knowing that Jackson hit his three famous 1977 homers off of Dodgers pitchers Burt Hooton, Elias Sosa, and Charlie Hough.

Jackson earned the nickname "Mr. October" for his heroics in the World Series, batting .450 in the 1977 Series and hitting five home runs in six games. In Game Six, he made history by hitting three homers in a row, each on the first pitch!

He led the Bombers to their first championship since 1962.

In 1978, the Yankees trailed the Red Sox by 14 games in July, but staged an amazing rally. After winning a one-game playoff over Boston, the Yanks won their second straight World Series. Ron Guidry was the pitching star, with a 25-3 record, a 1.74 Earned Run Average (ERA), and a Yankee-record 248 strikeouts.

The decade ended on a sad note when Thurman Munson was killed when a private plane he was piloting crashed. Munson, the first team captain since Lou Gehrig, was the heart and soul of the 1970s Yankees teams.

The Yankees reached the Series again in 1981, but it was their last high point for more than a decade.

The best
Ron Guidry, known as "Louisiana Lightning," won the Cy Young Award in 1978.

Sad day
The death of their leader, Thurman Munson, shocked the Yankees and their fans.

Happy day
Yankees lefty Dave Righetti threw a no-hitter at Yankee Stadium on July 4, 1983.

A new dynasty

No player on the New York Yankees was better during the 1980s than first baseman Don Mattingly, who won the league batting title in 1984 and was the 1985 MVP. That season, Mattingly set records for most grand-slam home runs in a season (6) and for hitting at least one home run in eight consecutive games. "Donnie Baseball" was also a slick fielder, winning nine Gold Glove Awards for fielding excellence.

Fiery skipper
Former Yankee player Billy Martin was hired and fired five times as the Yankees' manager.

Unfortunately, Mattingly played most of his career on losing teams. In his rookie season of 1982, the Yankees had their worst record (79–83) in 16 years.

By 1989, the Yankees sank to their worst finish in 22 years, and in 1990 they dropped to last place with the club's worst record since 1913.

Between 1982 and '91 Steinbrenner changed managers 11 times. From 1982 to 1994, the Yankees did not win a division title. "For a lot of clubs, 13 years without being in the postseason is no big deal," said Steinbrenner. "But for the New York Yankees, it is unacceptable."

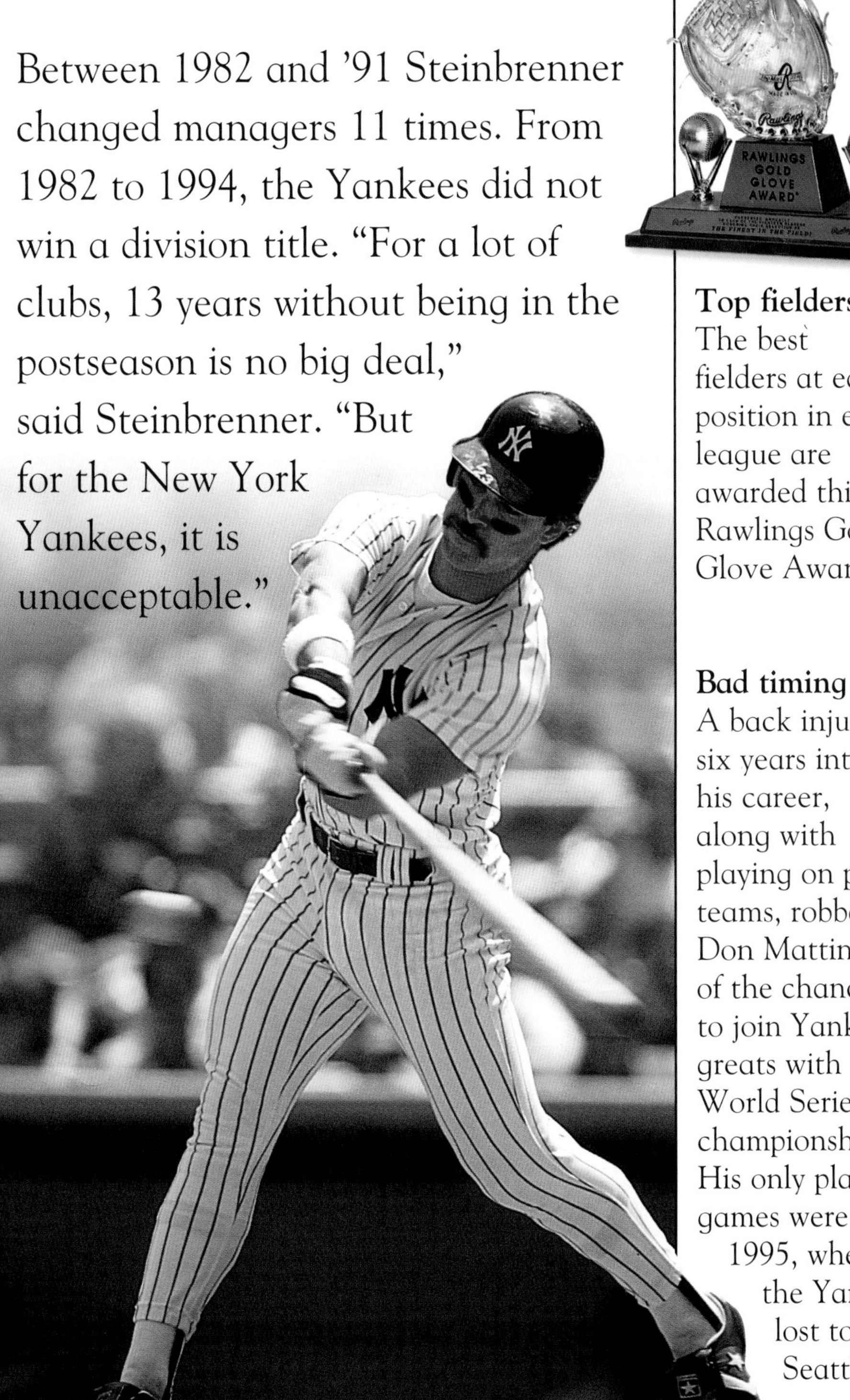

Top fielders
The best fielders at each position in each league are awarded this Rawlings Gold Glove Award.

Bad timing
A back injury six years into his career, along with playing on poor teams, robbed Don Mattingly of the chance to join Yankees greats with World Series championships. His only playoff games were in 1995, when the Yanks lost to Seattle.

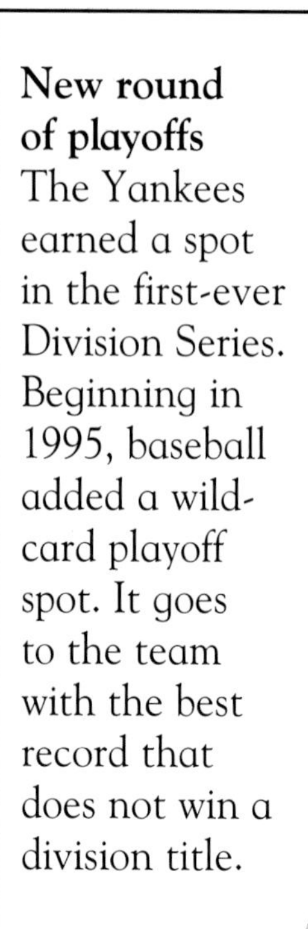

New round of playoffs
The Yankees earned a spot in the first-ever Division Series. Beginning in 1995, baseball added a wild-card playoff spot. It goes to the team with the best record that does not win a division title.

Multitalented
Bernie Williams is a great baseball player and also a great classical guitar player.

The winning spirit finally returned in 1995. Manager Buck Showalter's team won the wild card, but lost a playoff series to the Seattle Mariners.

Steinbrenner made another move and hired Joe Torre as the new manager. The former MVP catcher led a different type of Yankees team. Instead of relying on sluggers and home runs, these teams were built on pitching and defense.

Tino Martinez took over for Mattingly at first base, joining a solid nucleus of young stars.

Rightfielder Paul O'Neill was as intense as his swing was sweet. Bernie Williams filled the shoes of Mantle and DiMaggio in centerfield while spraying line drives from both sides of the plate.

The pitching staff would become the backbone of the Yankees. Left-handed pitcher Andy Pettitte joined ace David Cone in the starting rotation and won 21 games in just his second big-league season. Second-year reliever Mariano Rivera was the team's closer. He blazed fastballs past batters at an astonishing pace, striking out 130 batters in 107 innings.

New leader
The playing experience of Joe Torre (in jacket) as a catcher helped him work with the Yankees' pitching staff and mold it into one of baseball's best.

Mound star
From 1995 through 2002, Andy Pettitte won more games than any other A.L. lefty.

Series souvenir This pennant honors the Yankees on the occasion of their twenty-fourth World Series title.

Jump for joy! David Wells became the first Yankee to throw a perfect game since Don Larsen in 1956. Amazingly, Wells's New York teammate David Cone matched the feat the next season.

To complete the team, Torre inserted rookie shortstop Derek Jeter into the starting lineup in 1996. It proved to be a brilliant move, as Jeter earned Rookie of the Year honors and led the Yankees to their first World Series title since 1978. They defeated the N.L.-champion Atlanta Braves in six games.

The Yankees were now Jeter's team, and in his first six seasons, Jeter's Yankees won five American League pennants and four World Series championships.

The Yankees had a storybook season in 1998. They clinched a playoff spot in August—the earliest ever—and established an A.L. record with 114 regular-season wins.

Shining in the Series
By the time he was 25 years old, Derek Jeter had won four World Series titles and was among baseball's all-time leaders in a number of postseason batting categories.

Unlikely star
Yankees third baseman Scott Brosius was the MVP of the 1998 Series after hitting .471 with two homers and six RBI.

They steamrolled through the playoffs, too, setting a new major league record by winning a combined 125 total games. It marked the Yankees' seventh sweep and twenty-fourth world title.

The prize
Players who win World Series titles each receive a special ring, often covered with diamonds. This is Derek Jeter's 1999 Series ring.

Citywide
The 2000 Series was called "the Subway Series" after New York's underground transit system.

Expectations were high in 1999 and the Yankees did not disappoint. They won 98 games and swept the Series for the second straight year, this time against the Braves. Future Hall of Famer Roger Clemens won the deciding Game Four to give the Yankees their twenty-fifth title of the century.

The 2000 Series was Jeter's showcase as he hit .409 and was the Series MVP.

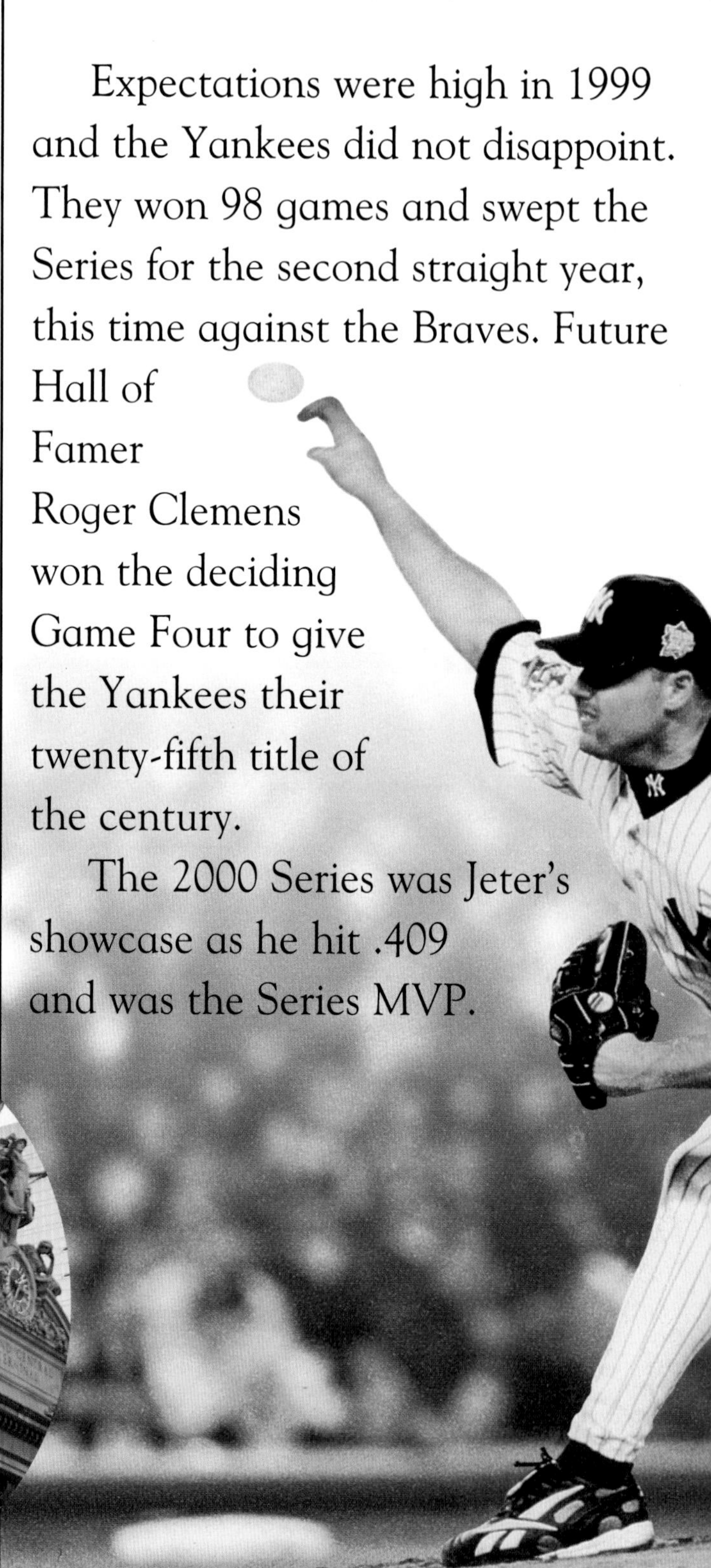

The Yankees won the first "Subway Series" since 1956 in five memorable games against the New York Mets. The club became the third Yankees team—and just the fourth team in history—to capture three or more World Series titles in a row. Clemens pitched two-hit ball over eight scoreless innings before Mariano Rivera sealed the victory and the championship.

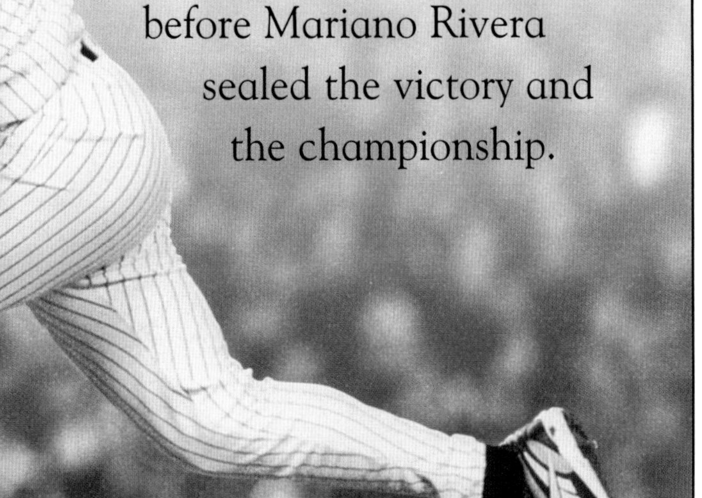

Clutch closer
Mariano Rivera has been nearly perfect in Series play. He has the all-time record with eight saves.

The Rocket
Roger Clemens won a record five Cy Young Awards with Boston and Toronto, but no Series titles. With New York, he added a sixth Cy Young and two Series rings.

The 2001 season was an emotional one. A national tragedy occurred on September 11, 2001, when terrorists attacked the United States, most horribly in New York.

When baseball resumed play, Yankees fans rooted for their team to represent New York's ability to rebound from adversity. The Yankees faced the Arizona Diamondbacks in the Series.

New man
After winning the 2001 A.L. MVP with Oakland, Jason Giambi signed with the Yankees, giving the team another superstar player.

Series stunner
Tino Martinez rounds third after hitting a game-winning homer in Game Four of the 2001 Series.

As America cheered, the Yankees staged some miracle comebacks. Down to New York's final out in Games Four and Five, Tino Martinez and Scott Brosius each hit game-tying, two-run home runs with two outs in the bottom of the ninth.

Unfortunately, New York then lost two straight in Arizona. Despite that heartbreaking defeat and the disappointment of a 2002 playoff loss, the Yankees' future looks bright. With new stars such as Jason Giambi and Alfonso Soriano, the Bronx Bombers should be among baseball's best for years to come.

We remember
Baseball joined all of America in honoring the victims of the 2001 terrorist attacks.

The latest star
Dominican-born Alfonso Soriano is the latest in a long line of Yankee stars. In 2002, he became the third player with 40 homers and 40 steals in one season.

Glossary

adversity
Obstacles or problems that one has to overcome.

American League (A.L.)
One of the two groups of teams that make up the Major Leagues.

amyotrophic lateral sclerosis (ALS)
A disease of the nerves and muscles that can cause paralysis and death. Also known as Lou Gehrig's Disease.

broadcaster
A person who works in radio or television, usually talking about whatever is being shown.

colonel
A military rank one level below the highest rank of general.

dependability
The ability to be trusted that one will accomplish a task.

dynasty
A group of people that maintains power or leadership over a long period of time.

free agent
A player not under contract to a particular team. He can offer his services to any team.

hurler
Nickname for a pitcher; to hurl means to throw.

jell
To come together.

Most Valuable Player (MVP)
An award given each year to the player in each league deemed as contributing most to the success of his team.

National League (N.L.)
One of the two groups of teams that make up the Major Leagues.

no-hitter
A game in which a pitcher starts and finishes the game without allowing the opposing team any hits.

nucleus
The center of an atom; a person or group of people of central importance.

pennant
A triangular piece of cloth, often covered with writing, awarded to the winners of a division or league in baseball. The term is also used to describe a division or league championship.

perfect game
A game in which a pitcher allows no base runners of any kind and starts and finishes the game.

persuaded
Convinced by using argument and speech.

save
Usually, a pitcher who finishes a game that his team wins after he comes in with men on base is said to have "saved" the game. He receives a statistical credit for that save. There are other situations, too, in which a pitcher can receive a save

sultan
A name used for a king or leader of some Arab countries.

tape-measure
A nickname for a very long home run, coming from the fact that these long hits are often measured.

wild-card
A term for a baseball team that enters the playoffs with the best record of all teams that did not win a division.